The Unapologist Reader

3 Poets: Steve Smart, James Jackson, Howard Firkin

First published 2010 by The Unapologist Press

www.unapologists.org

All rights reserved.

All material on these pages is copyrighted by its authors. No part of these pages, either text or image may be used for any purpose other than personal use: reproduction, modification, storage in a retrieval system or retransmission, in any form or by any means, electronic, mechanical or otherwise, for reasons other than personal use, is strictly prohibited without prior written permission.

© Copyright 2010 Smart Jackson Firkin

ISBN: 978-0-9808304-0-8

Table of Contents

The Unapologist Manifesto 1
Steve Smart 3
    Dollar Short 5
    Thought 6
    The Inner-romantic 7
    Hanged Over 8
    Sustain 9
    Vein 10
    Fucking Poet 12
    In and Out Again 14
    Onarock 17
    Poems and Open Doors 19
    Break Neck 21
    Shopgun 24
    Later Grows The Night 26
    One Night In Fairyland 27
    Less The Predator 29
    A Strange Profession 31
    The Last Night 33
    This, Our Winter 36
    Career Poet 38
James Jackson 39
    Chloe 41
    Pipedreams 44
    The Boy Who Drowned 46
    Dead Crow on the Beach 47
    Scenes from the Last Days 48
    (untitled) 51
    Big Brother Isn't Watching You 52
    Kristalltag 54
    Two Minutes Hatefuck 55
    These Boots are Made for Walkin' 56
    Anthem for a Bored Youth 58
    Hello Possums 59
    Hundred Year Storm 60
    the outer suburbs special school teacher 61
    G'Day Pentridge 62
    Alien 64

- Alone in the Northland Food Court ... 66
- Crowned ... 67
- Cunt Road ... 69

Howard Firkin ... 73

- Prayer of a brick ... 75
- Longitude ... 76
- Anzac Day 2009 ... 77
- Cuneiform ... 78
- Vacuum Clean ... 79
- Shadow Poem ... 80
- No wonder ... 81
- Imperfectly heard love song ... 82
- My life in amber ... 83
- A Thousand Things ... 84
- A Visit to the Comic's Lounge ... 85
- You ... 86
- My lover's lover's name ... 87
- A Landing At Sunset ... 88
- God loves us ugly ... 89
- I Contact ... 90
- It's Pez ... 91
- Cathedral of Venus ... 92
- Christmas Adam ... 93
- My House ... 94
- The Sugar Generation ... 95
- Today ... 96
- Forever ... 97
- Tow Truck ... 98
- When you're serious about love ... 99
- Fourteen self-explanatory lines ... 101
- Firkin's first space walk ... 102
- Sleek ... 103
- The sculptor's model remembers herself ... 104
- One last poem ... 105

The Unapologist Manifesto

Poetry is created in every society, in every language, in every circumstance. It has existed as long as human language.

We declare ourselves unapologetic upholders of the tradition of poetry and stand willing to defend it against fashion, trends, funding bodies, councils, schools, governments, bureaucrats, academics, and public opinion.

We call on all poets to raise their voices in support of their craft and their fellow poets.

We are not creating something new – we are registering our allegiance to something that has always existed. We invite all who refuse to apologise for a belief in poetry to join us.

Lives lived as poets are extraordinary lives.

www.unapologists.org

Steve Smart

Steve Smart is something of a cult figure in spoken-word circles. This limited success is very gratifying to him and has taken many years to achieve. Along the way he has performed his work thousands of times, travelled the globe, self-published often (chapbooks and CD's), and also once directed a poetry festival for six years. He has a strong presence online and is proud to be an Unapologist.

Dollar Short

If I had a dollar
for every time
someone's tried to kill me,
I'd be as broke as I am now

However

If you are planning
to hasten my demise
might I recommend
shooting me in the back
so I don't see the bullet coming

I do so love surprises

Thought

Can't bear the thought
of not being able to
bear the thought

Can't find the words
that describe why the words
are so important
and this is the rub . . .

Fortune and fame
the poet craves not these things
we're just trying to
understand ourselves well enough
to function as human beings

You ask what I do
this is the secret
       in a nutshell
I wallow in self-absorption
Trying to figure out why
I am the way that I am

This self-absorption
leads me to despise myself
and this self-despising
leads me to try
to figure out why I am
the way that I am

Finally there is the poem
that explains none of it
but gives a sense of purpose
and the purpose being found
more poems must follow
lest the purpose
should be lost

The Inner-romantic

The romantic in me
won't take a hint
can withstand
any beating I dish out
choke him, slap him
he just keeps on grinning
like there's something to be happy about
anticipating the next flight of fancy
all hearts and flowers
young Liz Taylors and mint juleps

ridiculous

My inner romantic
doesn't have the sense
God gave a grapefruit
still I can never bring myself
to evict him completely
always leave a key out
where I know he'll find it and
if some days I wish he'd just take a hike
leave me to my cigarettes and self-pity
I still believe deep down
in that romantic in me

ridiculous of course

Hanged Over

It's the skull cave-in

Hand-shakes all round
one drink turns into
the monster that ate my senses

Dear God, what did we do, again?

Wish I could think of something beautiful
         struggle for pleasant

Get me off this train

My head is a bullet wound and
this day will not improve
I think optimistically

Sustain

This beer will end
I'll leave this town
catch a gust of wind
to anywhere
forget my own existence

All I'll remember
is the old man
singing to himself
at the urinal
a quietly joyous sound

Lifted my spirits and I
consider it a lucky day
small moments of beauty
can sustain
a whole life

Vein

Wish that I had
something new to tell you
a secret to reveal
a joke you haven't heard
a theory we could
argue over 'til daybreak

That I could use simple words
to send the shiver down your spine
your lower back each vertebrae
into your . . .
                let's say toes

Wish I could take away
the things that make you
chew your nails down to the quick
crease your eyes with apprehension
when life is all missing lovers
and John-Travolta-film disappointing

Wish I could explain
why it's important
to never give up
on all those dreams we sang
so feverishly, drunk and mad

I wish I was
the person you called
when the words are too much
the silence never enough
the blood too
fucking fast
the dawn too
fucking far

All I can say
is I'm still here
still writing
like I promised I would
still trying to
figure it all out
so when you ask
I'll be able to explain
why we wish so hard

Fucking Poet
(for Sandy)

You called me a fucking poet
I took the compliment
return it one hundred fold

this does not make me
a better person
a better poet

the fact that you have left us
does not make me stronger or greater
you did that already

you brought me to my feet –
if I am a better person
it's because you believed I was

this is not about words
not grist for the mill
though the words come
will come still and again

we were more than the sum
of our words we were
tickling and giggling
stony silences followed by
teary embraces and more giggling

we were falling asleep
within minutes of each other
while the video played on

we were too much
to explain in such a short time
perhaps ever to be able
and still there is laughter
because you were a nut and so was I

Am, Am, Am
alright am
and you are a nut
are ya happy?

and this is written with all my love
because I'm a better nut
for the nut you are –
you me, us nuts

you said you couldn't see
dog shit in the dark
but then you said you were
learning to see with your eyes closed
what am I to think?

I work on my line structure
you continue to edit –
this poem is not finished

In and Out Again

Love meant hard work
one of us had to change
and why the hell should it be you?
Change work-suffer-suspect
the more jealous you are the more you love
no trust in the equation
I couldn't earn it
couldn't get it back if it were ever there
like so much breath it only appeared
after it was already gone

Relationships should be hard work you said
I didn't believe you
didn't know how hard it would get
never thought love should be war
finally saw the writing appear like lemon juice
the haggard cliché we had become
and so I walked away
it was never my intention to seem so cold

I understand it now I think
part of me at least is sorry
there were things you wanted
I could have given but didn't
still I didn't leave at the first sign of trouble
when you screamed and ranted
when you lashed out and struck me . . .
not trying to play the innocent
I was always as guilty as any

Still there was passion once
there was laughter I remember
we were so enthusiastic
suddenly there was only anger

yet you sought to persevere
love and hate so close sometimes
you did not want to lose
to have to start all over again
somehow it would be better
if we just tried harder, suffered more

I believed it for a moment
tried to give you what you wanted
you threw it back in my face
said I was *just using words*
that there was nothing behind them
perhaps you were right –
this is not about blame or recrimination
this is about letting go the past

This is about trying to understand
how it is that what I saw as love
could leave behind so scarcely a trace
barely a memory, a whisper at best
as if the wind just took it
blew it further than I ever thought to search
and what if I was wrong
that what I thought was love was never?

Follow the path to
never try to love again
or worse
never really believing –
there have been so many times
I have been wrong
know that I have also been right
have found one who makes me think
perhaps I should never again need question

There is a streak of idealism
would not dare
call myself poet if there weren't

I do not hate, am not bitter
simply a collection of regrets
many nights that never became lifetimes
a lifetime lived in such a short time
some days I hope but do not expect
some days all I hope for is hope

Onarock

A moment transcendent
marred by political density
doctrine overwhelming –
can we have a guilt free moment?

I question again my own
place, position, response
responsibility

Can't see a small naked child
standing on a rock
sun-drenched and at peace
with his universe, this ocean
without internal justification

Damnation
don't stare
wonder of life swamped by
potential thought crime

Can not the child be beautiful
Have we become so afraid?

In truth we have
and in this we have lost
even the appreciation of innocence
I am neither innocent
nor the monster
lurking outside the door

The child *is* beautiful
perfectly formed and at peace
his spirit not yet mocked
I am not at peace

can no longer view such beauty
without this sense of potential censure

Understand the foundation
the need to protect and yet
I find such sadness in
all that we have lost
all that we will take
from such a beautiful child
and replace with this
all consuming fear

Poems and Open Doors

The sign said open
but the door was locked
a sure sign that things had
already turned to burning crap

A brick through the window
situation desperate
note of apology, rushed but half sincere
the things you'll do when you really need a pen

No such thing as a victimless crime
minding your own business not always an option
I was trying to prevent a crime
or I was in a hurry . . .

I was thinking about something someone once said
that captured a moment in my life
I wanted to write it down before I forgot
it seemed of great importance

Moments are lost so easily
all the things I never wrote down

There's a certain sense of desperation to it all
I accept I may have been hasty
a poet without a pen is just a brain on legs
I never claimed to be rational

The sign said open
I was confused
the rock was handy
it was Autumn

Steve Smart

Without structure an open door is just air
the sign said open
the rock was thrown through air
yet there was structure
the crime was committed
the pen found
the poem written as confession
the poet sentenced to hang

Pause to argue semantics:

'If I reduced the poem to a sentence
would you reduce the sentence of the poet?'

the verdict revised, the poem thus reduced to
In Autumn I had a thought

Break Neck

Breaking necks
Bloody knows? Nose?

This is not
intrinsically hateful
just more angst -
'Patheticism' as a critical medium

You never tried to explain
why I couldn't use those words
you couldn't teach
what you didn't understand
Can you learn understanding?

I was demanding
I wanted to be taught
without your arse in my face
without your opinions
being rammed down my throat

I became reactionary but thoughtful
set out to never hurt anyone
then used bricks in psychic defence
Careful they said, *you may wake up*
and find yourself a poet
in this land of no metaphors

So be blunt.
Forget what you didn't learn.
Concentrate on what you know.
Never! use exclamation marks!
to disguise the fact
that there are words missing
and don't talk to *me* about futility

Prise open the prize
feign surprise at what you find
shrug and walk away
in secret glee wondering
at how lucky you can be

It didn't have to rhyme you know
it never has to do anything
      that's the secret
the rules were made
to be head-butted
the man said and I believed him
I always believed him
I always believe everyone
that's half my trouble
I even believe myself some days
though not today

Today I'm downloading porn
on a dead man's credit card
lying through my teeth
which are slightly broken:
perhaps the bricks I threw
bounced back and
hit me in the face

      It's a stunt at best
a not so clever disguise
an allusion to the lack of depth
the absence of structure
without guilt though still perhaps
dissatisfaction

You ask me what it means
I say I'm making it up as I go along
same as it's always been
I learn little and speak too much

wisdom from Fantail wrappers
supermarket tabloids
10 year old back issues of Rolling Stone

There's a brutality to the language
a li'l sugar on a rusty nail
carbon dated somewhere around
the point of learning that words
can be effective weapons
in the War Against Your Own Terror

Ah but that's just a little smug, ja?
Too many catchphrases;
paraphrasing propaganda
has been done to death
yet still we continue, claiming originality

I am the bastard child of the Unbeaten Poets
referencing things I half-remember
half-understand
I am not clever
I am simply determined to find a point
to all of these words inside my head

Steve Smart

Shopgun

It took 10 years and 15 days
and this is what I came up with
you might not think it's much to look at
it might not compare to the lack of nudity on television
or the screaming idiots surrounding us at every billboard

We're coming up for an election
vote for the biggest the best
the lie that you'd most *like* to believe

I didn't realise it would hurt so much
filling a ballot with tears
could it be that I was wrong?
that I was the *One* who was wrong?
that I just didn't grasp the subtleties of modern life
and I'm grumpy because I'm out of touch?

I don't know the latest hit song
I don't understand the popularity of anything
most specifically that band with the lead singer who sounds
very much like too many other lead singers
only with less charisma

I remember when charisma was a selling point
before selling became the ultimate selling point

I'm not throwing stones or implying shadows
I'm going to work for the man
the little man who lives inside you subconscious
I hear he pays well but isn't much for loyalty
that's ok though right? that's ok though right?
it's ok because values are outdated

I tell the best lies   trust in the lack of
I am the bright colours   trust in the lack of
I am the shiny packaging   trust in me

I am the one you've been waiting for
I am not the devil (unless you want me to be)
            tell me what floats your boat
I am not the devil I'm just the guy who saw the opening in the market
busted that hole wide and now I'm selling you your personality
cleverly disguised and on sale for everything you'll ever earn
does that make me the devil?
it doesn't matter
nothing matters
except that you believe everything I tell you

I wouldn't lie
I would lie
I wouldn't lie
I would lie

confused?
don't think
it will go away
just close your eyes
and imagine the world
as it must have been 10,000 years ago
now sliiiiiiiiiiide the gun into your mouth
sliiiiiiiiiiide the gun into your mouth just
sliiiiiiiiiiide the gun into your mouth and
shop you fucker
shop

Later Grows The Night

Where were you when the kissing stopped?

Me? I was drunk and passed out
I was there when it started
I was conscious, vaguely lucid
not quite sober and frankly not involved

I skulked around the peripheries
pretending to be invisible:
sat in the kitchen for a while
directing strangers to the toilet
until I spied with my little eye
something beginning with 'V' and ending in 'odka'

All the while the kissing continued
mouths on mouths, tongues on tongues
saliva being exchanged by the bucket load,
still the only thing my mouth connected with
was a bottle of Smirnoff

Later and later the night did grow
until the bottle was empty and I was full . . .
of shit mostly

I woke in the asparagus patch
about seven hours later
and the kissing had stopped
I'd missed it again
while someone, somewhere
was still staggering around, muttering

Where's me fuckin' vodka?

To no one in particular

One Night In Fairyland
(For Paris)

Just to be close to such pointless fame
I'd give it all to you
drag my knuckles on the ground
        I wanna be fashionable
                I wanna be ridiculous
                        I wanna be on the cover
of *Who? Weekly*
but you've never heard of me
my family doesn't own any islands
film studios, banks, hotels or large urbanised cities
there are no fake Romanian kings in my blood-line
and I never bought my way into a fancy university
only to leave under a cloud of rumours and innuendo

Still I feel I have much to offer
we could be so pointless together
you could explain handbags and backstage passes
and I could write poems on your abdomen
you could feel so safe –
I don't even own a video camera
I'd never make you feel stupid or like a tramp
a slut or a cartoon character
we could travel the world being impossibly glamorous
snorting cocaine and eating out your friends
stealing from expensive shops just for laughs . . .
I could change my name to Belarus or Stuttgart

I can change!
I could be as asinine as you'd want me to be
if only you'd look my way just once and see
that I am not clever or interesting
I can be as much of a jerk
as it will take to make you happy

or unhappy if that makes you happy
oh teach me how to be more like you
all fake smiles and vacant eyes
I'd write you a thousand lies
each less believable than the last
if you would only let me share a little of your world

Alas, 'tis never to be
they'll never let me into your clubs
your rat-thing would bite me
your boyfriends would beat me up for breathing your imported air
your family would ban me from all their overpriced hotels
and *Who* would write scandalous articles
claiming you had me arrested for stalking
but I would never hurt you
I offer love without judgement, devotion, self-abasement
I could be your night in shiny ugly clothes
just put me in your purse

I wanna be your dog

Less The Predator

I am less predatorial
than you might think
I have been prey
I used to pray to be preyed upon
I was too shy
I am shy still

I have had more sex than some
much less than many
somewhat less than I could have had
if I had have tried . . . harder
know the palm of my hand
like the back of my hand
from all those nights I waited and hoped

I learned to speak
thought conversation would be important
then had to learn how not to speak
when I became the guy you had
intense conversations with
before you went and fucked someone
who was more fun

I am too much
in my own head but I am not the
awkward child I was
I've been around
oh baby I've been around
I could show you a map
draw you a bath

I am more comfortable than I have
ever been inside in my own skin
I could tell you stories

we could go dancing
drink 'til dawn
get the giggles like children
I don't want to be
intense like I can be

I want to be your first smile
in the morning
your last smile at night
want to be the thing
that makes you laugh like a nut
when everything else in your life
is conspiring to make you cry

I don't want to be
intense like I can be
I want to be the guy
who is more fun –
I'll show you my map
if you show me yours

A Strange Profession
(for Eddie Vedder)

I question my
place in the universe
the way in which I live
destructive patterns sometimes overwhelm
never questioned what I am
the importance of poetry
to tell the stories
to keep score
somehow

And you taught me
I could tell those stories
without having to be so literal
without always having to name the
names, dates, times, places
mix the fiction and fact
to find the truth
I've tried to be
honest

A strange job
we both well know
your stage is much larger
the intent remains the same
to sink into the unfathomable
to reach the heart of a world that
seems intent to rid itself of simple joy
to speak in a voice loud enough to wake
the heaviest sleeping conscience of man
slap it awake crying *we are still here*
right where we've always been
our job has not changed

All I want to say
is my name is not important
if we never meet we are still part
of the same fight against denial
the words we write, our best defence
I always felt kin to you
your voice resonates
deep within me
still

The Last Night

It feels somehow like I've
used up all of my nights

A strange thought
to be left with only days

Moved too fast
this constant rushing

Days at slower pace
energy at lower ebb

Nights picking up
where they left off
rising to flood too quickly
storm in a glass, overwrought, overblown

I'm trying to tell you I may have
drowned without realising
washed up on the shore
of some faraway pond

I know I'm not being clear
God knows I know that

If I could paint or sing
it might make more sense
just some days I get frightened
confused can't find my place in it all

Some days I am
a broken thing
all the glue won't mend
all the words won't solve

Simply I have been
too often indulgent
certainly I have been indulged
not always held to account

I am too much a child
though not perhaps the child I was
Allan Ginsberg said
I have become another child
and I take him out of context
I was so determined to reach adulthood

They say it's my generation
a refusal to grow up
what should I believe –
that I resist
or am simply incapable?

Search for the elusive third option
but find myself too often distracted

Instead of being liberated
by myriad of choices
options available
paths of least or most consideration
I feel weighed down
one idea bounds into the next
I cannot settle
there are too many words
behind which to hide

Strip them away

Slow these thoughts

Leaving will not fix anything

A quiet space

One solid decision at a time

Stop having last wines

What do I need?

What can I not live without?

One sentence to replace a thousand

I think know
what you would say
if you were here

This, Our Winter
(for Ian McBryde)

I have trawled the streets
of Berlin and Belfast in January
been lost in New York at 5am
with the temperature below zero
smoked outside bars
in Montreal in the snow
and come August I have listened
to people from all those cities
complain about the cold in Melbourne

It's a different kind of cold here
gets deep into your bones
no one sees our winter coming
until it cannot be avoided
no international reputation precedes it
but this is Austraaaalia they cry
we were told it never got cold here
to which we reply with proximity
to Antarctica

I say again this is a winter city
built under looming shadows
the logic of bluestones
gothic buildings and heated courtyards
dark colours to belie cheery moods
we may complain but we prefer it this way
to the hell of high summer
when every exit is an
oven door waiting too be opened

You will find us
when the fog sets over Eltham
Belgrave shivers at the foot of the hills
St Kilda wraps against the North wind
Sunshine shelters from the downpour
and Fitzroy hides in her tiny bars
till spring relief
then summer swelter
in this, our winter come again

Career Poet

When poetry becomes work
leave it alone
do something else
you kill the things you love
by confusing them with responsibility
making them chores
with punishments for tardiness

When you haven't read a poem in months
because it feels like you could get it wrong
that you mightn't read it well enough
while you're only writing poems
because you've told people you're a poet
and you hate to be a liar
or unemployed
leave it alone

The responsibility
is to never lose the joy
you first found in those first lines
the moment of awakening
the moment of creation
the moment you discovered that you were
as so many before you
but not quite like any of them

James Jackson

James Jackson is the self-proclaimed "Monster of Poetry" and one of the most controversial Melbourne poets of recent years. A former professional wrestler, musician and actor, Jackson performs poetry wherever will still book him. These performances often contain confrontational elements which have divided his fellow poets and poetry audiences alike. You have been warned.

Chloe

So I was walking down Flinders Street the other day
and I could have dropped in to see Chloe
but I thought, "What's the point?"
surrounded now as she is
by oafish, footy-tipping salarymen
each another layer of cellulite
on her once stunning, naked skin
drunkenly hating, knocking, breaking her
because she could never belong to them, but that said,
they wouldn't know what to do with her if she did
at a Broady bus stop she now sits
Dimmeys tracksuit, cracked Peter Jackson lips, screaming kid

That place where I used to skate
then go below to the café
where the food was cheap
on the razor's edge of the used by date
and the subterranean Hurstbridge line
wedged in the crowded carriage was I
between pretty McRob girls astute in the arts
of quickening the beats of schoolboy hearts
that place is now Federation Square
a remarkable, modern monument
to what, I'm not sure
where skating is strictly prohibited
by simpering security guards
where there is no cheap café, only 7-11
where the food has the right date
and if it doesn't you can sue them

So I go through the Flinders Street concourse
try to do the loop and end up
getting off at some place called "Southern Cross"
because I'm completely lost

and to be honest I don't know where these names come from
to me it sounds
like Top of the Town, Daily Planet and Southern Cross
just as fucked, ugly and soulless

So somehow I locate Collins Street
find to my horror I'm mired among
assholes on their way to clubs
sporting haircuts like the kids in Beyond Thunderdome
as above what those kids would have called "skyrapers"
seem to sprout like plants on time lapsed film
while security cameras record me
sit at a bus stop seat,
and watch a Melbourne sunset
but fail to see even half the story
as I admit with grief
not even the glorious sky we lie beneath
can ever hope to bring relief
from the mean-spirited monotony
of this city we have been bequeathed
and some forty year old tradie
from Patterson Lakes
walks past me with his paper-bag-job lay
and shoots me a look of utter disdain
as if how dare I disgrace his retinas
with an image he can't immediately place

So I end up at a club for someone's birthday
hearing how so-and-so's girlfriend lost all that weight
and how between them they're raking in 200K
and you would think for that money
they'd have something interesting to say
while the music is so loud I couldn't hear them anyway
let alone hear myself think
convenient, because if you had access to logic
the first thing you would do is get up and leave
but partly inured by gold-plated booze
I feign attention as people speak personally

and personably of and among themselves
and other superficialities
when finally released
I walk into the street
a bouncer says, "no pass outs, mate"
"I'm not coming back," I reply
crack a smile as wide as his
and take to the city night

Pipedreams

the decrepit, senile uncle
Northland no longer talks to
sat me on his knee
for longer than was necessary
it is supposedly fun
and I thought it would be;
leisure was once his middle name
before it changed
for reasons yet unattained
to Pipeworks Fun Market
yet we were not amused
there among my own surely
I should have been happy?
but the store-holders bore the drawn shoulders
of those who have waited too long
for wins, kings, the apocalypse or bargains
and have known for years they should stop holding on
while trying to hock their ex-Op Shop stock
I asked how much for the plastic-framed print of Mad Max III
fifty
the informal economy of language rationed
Aunty
would thrive in a place like this
and I can see Masterblaster at the gates
collecting the $2 parking fee
today Australia's first bungee tower
besieged under a north-easterly
totters desolate
bereft of every mullet and fluorescent *Lightening Bolt* singlet
that used to validate it
and I wondered if anyone ever buys anything
the customers seeming to have the same ken
as those trying to sell it to them
perhaps it is just an escape

and as I sped away
from that place
it seemed pipedreams, all
we had seen
enough
and now we were awake

The Boy Who Drowned

Beneath the brown
lie the bones
of the boy who drowned
years ago now

three wagged school
to go for a swim
two came up again

screams were heard
by our neighbour –
a trained lifesaver
and mistaken for the sounds
of kids having fun

by the time she realised
something was wrong
he was gone
drowned
never to be found

pickled now
in truth serum
his flesh made food
for carp and eels
gone long since
the way of him

now new eels
wind around
his empty cage of ribs
as they would
dead tree branches
discarded tyres
any riverbed detritus

carp bite bare bones
futile nourishment

the boy groans
the river flows

Dead Crow on the Beach

Speckled now
by grains of time
helpless in the wind
death suspends the sands
and both hands
cease their twittering
the gusts that once
held him high
the pale shore which gripped his lustre
between the sky
now conspire
to drain him of all colour
we yearn to mourn
his stately span
or noble beak
but the reaper skews all beasts
horrid feet
justify the bleakness of his plan
talons upturned in the sand
driftwood from a distant tree

James Jackson

Scenes from the Last Days

The gangs do not take over the highways
traffic remains gridlocked
drivers wait to witness the cause of delays
only to find none is apparent
we parrot theories beyond our reckoning
and reach for the stars
in anachronistic shuttles
that may as well be horse and carts
we search for inhabitable planets
by shooting blanks in the dark
our sins are charted
and kept in filing cabinets on cards
by clerics primitive
as the great apes they decry
beguiling tapestries of cloud
occupy the sky
which are noted for the first time
it does not stop but speeds up
and slows down
as if to mock our clockwork
like premonitions
too much for the mind
bureaucrats go bankrupt
by fining themselves
and finding themselves
no more than another pound of flesh
on an already cannibalised corpse
desiccated blades of grass
snap underfoot
nature takes its course
it rains for days
gravediggers break spades on clay
hours decay
a conspiracy of sand and sea
reveals wrecks of ships unnamed
that never sailed

James Jackson

crowds gather to gawk on the beach
signals are discovered
from galaxies away
then fade before they can be traced
not from the news
the missing link dies
a decrepit troglodyte
cause of death—suicide
buried in an unmarked grave
by sentimental scientists from the CIA
furniture by IKEA rains from the sky
in what is called a clever marketing ploy
which they rightly deny
they know it wasn't them
and they are terrified
diaries bubble from landfills
white hot with honesty
but unsigned
doggerel litters train walls
graffiti causes an uproar
poetasters write PC crap
for grants from bureaucrats
poets in Air Max and caps
remain strapped for cash
art imitates life
and decays a little further each day
life imitates art
and stays exactly the same
we name this feeling
with an unspeakable noun
which only exists in text
typed into your phone
every night the sound of a machine
can be heard in each home
as if something has been left on
we wake in fright
to the slow interminable drone
craving for solitude grows
for boarded up windows

bunkers and tombs
while all we wish to exclude
we merely trap inside these rooms
many try to step off the globe
once they become certain they know
our times amount to little more
than a mediocre interlude
our bodies a complex concourse for water
our consciousness not enough electricity
to power a watch battery
who'd have thought it?
in the event of a blackout
we try to set the world on fire
but find it is already alight
just move towards it
and everything will be all right
it simmers first
like flesh fit to burst
a solitary molecule
a bubble
started this boil
and now it is done
we have become
a single unquenchable thirst

(untitled)

dead tree
wood squid
tendrils
tentacles

sere
on the park grass shore

waves wash in and out
we stop to look at it

storeys tall leviathan
horizontal across the oval

should be moved
there is nothing we can do

Big Brother Isn't Watching You

for Steve Smart

correct erectile function, more orgasms and longer lasting sex
is watching you
more vitamin B12, E12, D12, with anti-oxidants to kill free radicals
is watching you
the untold elation you will glean from owning the new Guy Sebastian
album
is watching you
while you are still not convinced letting lasers near your eyes is the
smartest idea in the world the money you *can* afford to spend on laser
eye surgery with Dr Rick Wolf
is watching you
around November the prospect of getting an autograph from a porn
star at Sexpo
is watching you
being in possession of a particular variant of health only applicable to
men and the magazine of the same name both of which seem to be
primarily concerned with the cultivation of highly visible abdominal
muscles is in no way homosexual but
is watching you
the advanced diploma you can score from a new institute which
accepts both Mastercard and Visa because you were too busy ripping
bongs in high school
is watching you
Hamish, Andy, Bridgette, Dave, Tom, Dylan, Dave, Dicko, Dave, Kate,
Dave, Dave, Dave, Dave, Dave, Jackie O, Dave, Kyle, Matt, Dave, Jo
and some other jumped up motherfucker you'd rather not know
is watching you
ironically, especially if you are a man, or, come to think of it, a woman,
the privacy of a women's-only gym
is watching you
the stunning cinematic experience of watching yet another fucking
movie based on yet another fucking comic
is watching you

don't look now but an emaciated African child with hungry eyes who
was probably a small boy soldier and knows how to handle an M5
is watching you
a higher, lower, fixed, long short term interest rate
is watching you
the only chance you will ever get to see those European guys who had
that one song on the radio play their laptops live in a set
encompassing every piece of music they have learnt since age nine
with the exception of that one song from the radio
is watching you
a choice of over four hundred specialty stores, six thousand parking
spaces and four food courts
is watching you
thinnest celebrity polls, sex tips, sealed sections and yet another
Hollywood diet filled with holes
is watching you
while you think you may be watching it, in fact more American
television about CSI, ER, NYPD, detectives in hospitals and serial
killers who are cops who are werewolves who are single who are
lesbians who are simple who are dancing who are ugly who are
beautiful who are so despicable they would snort the spilled coke out
of the red carpet through a improvised straw fashioned from a pilfered
piece of Perez Hilton's bog roll
is watching you
but Big Brother? That's right, Big Brother
isn't watching you

Kristalltag

Smithereens litter the pavement
put on your thongs or cut your feet
celebrating the nation means chucking your empties
wherever you feel slightly unsure
pitch them against a wall
and pretend you are Shane Warne
the threat of fire licks at our doors
but we were never much good
at taking a hint
we parade the stars of our sports
in the storm of ticker tape
there is no-one left to ask why
death squads roam the streets
in blue singlets that could be
black or brown, their plastic flags
flap flatly in the north easterly
most still in their teens
southern cross soldier
weekend warriors
reading *Zoo Magazine*
searching for those without a footy team,
individuals watering their gardens at the wrong time,
suspected arsonists
and anyone else
who wants to get lippy with us
to hand them over to the police
they leave their trails of broken empties
the sun blasts through a shard of broken glass into a pile of dry grass
a fire starts

Two Minutes Hatefuck

whole reefs of coral in reach
galaxies beneath the sea
the fragment once set in glass
a tiny crinkle in pink
now lying in the smithereens
a desiccated heart
it's a beautiful thing

what are the stars?
from the birth of the universe
the patient about to be
anesthetised upon the table
implores me "I've got a Masters degree
now get me a cup of tea"

fingers are held up
neither of us knows how many
our tandem maladies
interchangeably innocent
of moral or precedent
children play and say
today you can be O'Brien
and I'll be Winston
I could not give my friend his freedom

and is time no more
than a litany of betrayals
an abacus of days
a two minute hatefuck
ecstasy, confusion and pain
impotent to change

James Jackson

These Boots are Made for Walkin'

We make
the images screened
in the Ludovico Technique
and the two minutes hate
a true snuff movie
has never been discovered
existing only in our brains
a boot stamping on a human face
reliable
or not I remember a time
Kubrick's film
was only memories
screen shots in books
and a movie parody
in *Mad Magazine*
Solzhenitsyn was just another
bare bum in the shower
who couldn't come clean
present a filthy prisoner
and that's what will be seen
we assumed it was the OFLC
who had removed the strange fruit
the irony
was that Kubrick was cured
rendered terrified
at the sight
of his own work
under pain of death threats
and an upset guttiwuts
he made it go away
no government conspiracies
just a boot stamping on a human face
all the same
apparently Tony

never liked the film
his story came as a result
of his wife being assaulted
who says you can't make a difference?
violence
giveth and it taketh away
a boot stamping on a human face

Anthem for a Bored Youth

Fresh from hallowed halls of grammar school
they make their passage o'er the sea
barely more than boys and girls
they take the shores of Gallipoli

weary and weighed with heavy packs
uniformed in the latest fashions
armed with naught but minimal facts
they sit and drink their liquid rations

their ANZAC spirit mixed with coke
they proudly salute the standard
and search for reverence to evoke
tears at the grave of great grandad

then to the next stage of their Contiki campaign
they wander blankly to their waiting ride
stumble on the bus with chatter inane
drunk on national pride

what passing bells for those who live as cattle?
none, but there is no pauser to doubt
empties littering the Turkish soil
proved they had a Big Day Out

Hello Possums

A returned serviceman
his wife rife with Methodism
both overwrought
with post-war construction restrictions
built the house I live in

With fibro cement and good intentions
to create a nice place
where china ducks could fly free
without a hint of a motion

When it was common for Dads
to mow the lawn with a tie on
Saturdays after washing the Holden
then hiding in their sheds
smoking "Craven A's"
sweltering under the Australian sun
that burns brighter now
than it did in those days

I try to sleep in the bedroom
that had been their daughter's
when the nights revert
to pre-colonial quiet
I hear the satanic screeching
and the scratching
beneath the walls that provide
not a front or a behind
just an inside
where they reside
latent and oft-denied

I think about my mother
and what they called her
funny turns
then *nervous breakdowns*
and wonder if she too heard the possums

Hundred Year Storm

Then the city disappeared
Eradicated by cloud

The skyline strained
From the dark grey liquid

Eons waned
Back and forward

the outer suburbs special school teacher for finn at lunchtime they lock a three hundred pound seventeen year old boy in a cage called time out because he bit someone who may or may not have been a teacher who is counting at this stage he does not say much as usual teacher continues yard duty breaking up fights between students throw a few at him just because he is there they do not hate him any more than anyone else probably would not have taken the job is a job after all this time they actually like him not punching him in the mouth should be proof enough of that kid in the cage takes his shirt off round the back teacher sees and thinks he must be hot winter this year but this is ridiculous fights start again teacher runs in for another beating them would only end up getting him sued for what little he has got better things to do something weird in the cage boy is taking down his pants under the gaze of the rest of the yard he drops his jocks and redefines time out by starting to masturbate in the time out cage things have gone from bad to worse teachers do not have a clue what to do something some try to cover the other kids eyes teacher who notices this and tells them to get the other kids inside they tramp bemused teacher finds some old jackets from lost property of the special school anecdotes for this week this one will definitely make the staff meeting although maybe this time the staff will exercise a sense of decorum must be adhered to the cage door is opened teacher tells the wanker to cover himself with jackets and get out of the cage which was probably his intention now fulfilled he wanders out the windows the rest of the school look on as he is taken away by teacher leads him inside to the padded cell and locks it is time to return to yard duty beyond the school grounds are endless housing estates and new developments as far as the eye can see teacher there in the yard alone he takes an apple from his pocket gets in one bite and it starts to rain

G'Day Pentridge

seventeen at best when I did me first stretch
in Turana for stealing a Torana I confessed
unimpressed the judge said "now you're not a kid
pack up your shit and say G'day to Pentridge
rumour always had it jail was an occupational hazard
a networking opportunity with three meals and good security
but you can get a shiv in the ribs for a packet of cigs
or become a pig on the spit and bleed every time you shit
you say don't touch me – I know so and so on the outside
to cunts doing life who'd like a knife in the spine
try to have a quick snig over post pix of chicks from Number 96
and you can't get it up – all you see is dicks
every day you get in blues with gangs and screws
and bruised so bad blokes ask what happened to you
outward scars are nothing – you bleed internal
time is eternal in this infernal hell hole
shaver motor ball point pen and a needle
like you needed a reminder on your skin you been in
bluebirds and spiderwebs in never fading ink
I got out but they all knew I'd been in Pentridge

I tried to work but the nightmares got worse
me missus gave me some H to help me sleep at first
but me thirst was a curse I did burgs in the burbs
always needed one more hit just to calm my nerves
our daughter was born addicted like her parents
and then we had a son who died of cot death
I got pressed by standover men to start dealing
unfeeling cut the shit with anything I could find
one time I even used Strychnine
in Sunshine – ten ODs – all customers of mine
skipped town to avoid the heat in Glenrowan
me missus knocked off a Ned Kelly figurine
got busted – I said it was me – I didn't want her back in Fairlea
and the cops searched the car and found enough speed
and H and weed to kill a fucking footy team

that's when I knew I'd burnt me last bridge
and got ready once again to say G'day to Pentridge

I wasn't just imprisoned but put in H division
where every man was on a mission to be the most vicious
razor blades in the soap shivs made from toothbrush handles
a trip to the shower black could be fatal these vandals
of human flesh were the best crims in the state
ready to cave in your face with weights in a pillow case
Chopper played the same record every fucking day
We've got to get out of this place
and you watch rock spiders get sliced in broad daylight
and discuss the fucking Nazis with Julian Knight
and think about suicide while your mates get a knife
and decide which bits of themselves they'll cut off tonight
and somehow I survived it all and lived
to finish me stretch and say goodbye to Pentridge

twenty years on for old times' sake
I took a walk through this new housing estate
me tatts have faded but the memories stay
today I walk down the street and I'm hardly ruthless
just an old man on methadone and toothless
the truth is I'm useless – my life has been fruitless
they call it Pentridge Village – fuck me
most of the cunts living here wouldn't know what it used to be
the exercise yard is now some yuppies' front yard
a security guard trying to be hard
said; "it's private property – get out immediately"
and I saw red said "G'day Pentridge" and hit him in the head
which led I expect to the way he bled and next
I gave him a kicking he's not likely to forget
by the time the Jacks arrived he was spread on the cement
and with a flood of regret I realised I could never get
another sentence in Pentridge now a pretentious tenement
with Ronnie Ryan in me mind and Ned in me chest
I charged them fucking Jacks and let their guns do the rest

Alien

what surrounds us
cicatrix of consciousness
manifest otherness
the body
perpetual motion
of a piston
connected to nothing
tended by a bespectacled man in a tie
with a penchant for pouting
and panic
who continues for no reason
except following orders
must be followed in due course

while within
the avaricious
collector of truth
denies even a glimpse
of his treasure trove
wrinkled eye winks
he will take only your corpse
in exchange for what he knows
shelled as if by a child
leaves us grey mass
to desiccate and die
escargot
yet to be identified

and I would put it to you
they believe
our crafts crashed in their deserts
we take them in their sleep
for erotic experiments
sight unseen

they draw us
right out of all proportion
and little do we know it
some of them believe
we created their race
that we are so divine
we caused their evolution

Alone in the Northland Food Court

Throngs pass as
aeons pass
the moon
yet this is the solitude
of a satellite in orbit
they always said;
the world doesn't revolve around you
but perhaps it is on a loop?
like the lack of tune
forming a sound track
for the Sunglasses Hut
opposite
the girl sits
buried among endless lenses
and party music:
model as misanthrope
in an empty shop
peering at the passing freaks
from her niche
perhaps she, like but unlike me
now knows what it is to be lonely

Crowned

Our other friend had become lost
in translation of directions passed
on the loop he ended up at Melbourne Central
the museum of childhood
perhaps exhibited a still insurmountable obstacle
thought extinct yet rising megalithic
skeletal steel
smashed the cupboard to smithereens
lying at the feet of the bones
panicked by the height of buildings
and the backed up traffic
our friend fled for home

leaving us jewels in the Crown
Cinema Complex
arrangements of fellow encrustations
trying to shimmer as spoils of an empire
and only managing the cracked diamante glare
of treasure fit for a king
to sew on his Bedazzler
Like us, some were there to see *TMNT*
initials hiding the shame
of antiquated middle names
for these post graduate days
no-one, child or adult
is going to be entertained
by anything ninja or mutant
the imagination in modern animation for children forsaken
for colour and movement

Later bloated on nostalgia
we made our way from the cinema
trying to negotiate Crown's multilevel maze

having been born too late for a map of the layout to be emblazoned on
our brains
Flames! Greeted us outside
I saw Bartertown, *The Stand* and several other images
desperate as indebted gamblers
getting out of the red with their bodies
used to fuel the ostentatious blaze
illuminating freak flashes
of Southbank's malaise
grown strong since the days I used to skate that concrete
as an overgrown ham-fisted teen
aged cities such as this can spend decades
too old for Ninja Turtles
too young for urban sprawls
before finally awkwardly coming of age
embracing inner-city DINKS drinking Chardonnay,
the fray down at Crown gambling the life in their eyes away
thugs en route to clubs mute
save for what their fists can say
and every other experience of humanness
that makes a city change
yet I suspect we are safe
our Never-never Land is drinking cask wine from plastic bottles meant
for water
while eating pizza by the Yarra
as those clockwork fires blaze

Cunt Road

We had been to St Kilda Beach
and we were going to see my grandmother in Fairfield
that's why we didn't take the Eastern
and went up on Hoddle Street and
I was probably eating an ice cream
and my dad was driving
while some guy called Julian Knight
was in a pub drinking
and as we drove down that street
the ice cream sent a chill through my teeth
a sudden cold breeze
caused me to shiver
and in a matter of minutes we got there
and my grandmother said "You're late for dinner"
but just because I missed the Hoddle Street massacre by an hour
doesn't mean I don't love to begrudge Cunt Road
and they give it other names you know
it's futile like calling VDs STIs
confounding like commission flats are public housing
you can have your pretentious Nepean Highway and Hoddle Street
supposedly marking where suburbs meet
it's like saying the rest of Julian Knight is bad but he's got good feet
he might have made Hoddle Street famous and dangerous too
but that motherfucker is Cunt Road through and through
and can someone even begin
to try to tell me what suburb Cunt Road is in?
and don't give me this Abbotsford shit
that's a suburb that doesn't exist
started by an embarrassed bitch from Richmond
with her knickers in a twist
and I think I have shown
Cunt Road is a suburb all of its own
it's like when you're on the phone
"Where are you man?"

James Jackson

"I'm on Cunt Road!"
it's more Melbourne than grey skies and depression
and if you follow it south in a logical progression
you'll be bang on Frankston
but I'm betting that is a destination you find upsetting
so go north instead and you'll end up in Epping
and can you imagine living on Cunt Road?
I believe Chopper Read lived on Hoddle Street
but even he moved eventually
it might be convenient if your intent
was to sell sex or smack to pay the rent
or if you were sent to commence
intense community development
with a Cars That Ate Paris bent
even thought that is impossible
dudes sell their souls to the devil
to freeze the temperature gauge level
until they can turn
or get on the Eastern
because they know
if you break down on Cunt Road
giant skeleton hands
secrete from the concrete
and drag you and your car below
without a trace to be seen
before you interrupt the traffic flow
and don't try to harass
the City of Yarra's
spokesperson said;
"That is a fallacy
but in all actuality
it would serve to lessen congestion in the municipality"
like swerving to hit windscreen washers
it's Night of the Living Dead
and you too can be legend
but they only drop if you shoot them in the head
and don't open your window and think they're your friends
because they'll bite you instead

and you'll end up crazed, listening to 28 Days
later it will be you washing windscreens for change
staring down the barrel of a gun
mumbling "brains" and "I'll give youse a free one"
time so dour in peak hour
I was the passenger in this beast
driven by a speed freak
all of nineteen and snorting for three
with a thing for me
occasionally I wanted to jump her
but mostly I wanted to thump her
Cunt Road was bumper to bumper
we were more stationary than a ring binder
and the fire inside her was driving her wilder
inches became miles
Cunt Road had stopped time
she was right off her dial
it was her time of trial
because in her mind's eye she's passed one twenty-nine
spun a speed limit sign
with barely a sigh
she was feeling sublime
as she crossed the state line
we were settling into the Best Western and I
enjoyed Gundagi
and I thought she would die when she opened her eyes
only to find
we were still stuck in fucking Cunt Road
with nowhere to go

Howard Firkin

Howard Firkin has been writing, publishing, and performing his poetry since the mid nineteen seventies. This makes him either a precocious talent or the oldest of the unapologists by a long shot. His work has been praised, reviled, and ignored in very unequal measure by the leading lights of the Australian literary scene. Now it's your turn...

Prayer of a brick

Dear God, let me be missing, crumbled dust,
when others try to recreate this wall.
Let me have been the one which made it fall;
the fissured one that let the damp get just
a sweaty toehold in and kick it down.
You made me mortal, cunt. Well, fine. I'll die.
And you and nothing else will swirl about
not knowing time, and wearing nothing out,
and I won't be and won't have been, won't lie
for you, outline a never had been town.

And you, your brain can trace the molecules
that once were me, and know I was a brick,
and I'll deny it. Liar. Make more fools
and tell them. I'll deny it, God. You prick.

Longitude

(The lowest orbit)

Around and round we go and never find
an edge to fall off. Longitude's a con:
you're warmer, hotter, cooler, colder—gone.
Each new location only part defined,
although you've done the latitude before.
I don't remember ever being here.
I don't remember waking, wishing you
had used the name of somebody I knew,
and feeling flat as rings of last night's beer.
Another day reveals another shore.

Time is position. Check your watch. Replace
the figures. Plot each spot you orbit: low,
but regular as any mass in space.
I might see you around… (And round we go.)

Anzac Day 2009

(Zombie Diggers, attack!)

Rouse the lazy buggers from their bed!
We need them answering our endless call:
new generations want to see them fall
in mud, in grainy black and white, fall dead
and rise, like dawn, like tears in teenage eyes.
Oh they had guts all right, back then. They saw
their guts, exploded from torn bodies, wore
their insides out, died writhing, but died sure
that others came behind: there's always more.
The young are not our future: they're supplies.

Get up you lazy bastards! Up! No death
for you, no sleep, no quiet bird song, no
repose: resuscitation without breath.
We need you to enlist the next to go.

Cuneiform

Could anyone be bothered pressing these
in clay? Or scratching them in polished stone?
Words once were more than writing, were their own
Accomplishment—you didn't read at ease,
you read at work, you dragged them from a field.
Then words were stooked, hand-tied, and lined in rows.
You harvested whatever you could carry.
But now, each day's another dictionary,
a library of untranslated prose.
We weigh the chaff and think we're talking yield.

I don't believe there's anything to say
that someone reading this in 3010
might think was truly worth the waste of clay
except, "I was alive like you. Back then."

Vacuum Clean

Is this condition possible? I thought
a vacuum had to be an empty space?
I shouldn't even get to see the face
that's hanging in my mirror. This place ought
to be as clean as mortuary steel,
but this is empty of another kind:
it's object full but purpose empty, clean
of reason, free of knowing what you mean,
the blank of having nothing on your mind,
the space of having nothing left to feel.

All words resolve to facial gestures here—
no air to give them shape enough to call.
The time has come when everything is clear—
so clear you can't see anything at all.

Shadow Poem

These are not words. These are the shadows cast
when one meets zero. Binary. The light/
its absence. Binary. You cannot write
without a (power) point. Words must have passed
into the future when we weren't aware.
Words used to live in skin. Words used to smell
of printers ink, their pages stained with tea
or curried fingerprints. They used to be;
they were—there when the book was closed as well—
and now they're not. They're nothing: absenceware.

This only is a poem while you choose.
It lives like perfume on another's skin.
This poem leaves you nothing left to lose:
it ends whenever you decide: begin.

No wonder

I'm fading: faster than my hair grows grey;
I'm washing left too long out on the line;
I'm last night's salad—look, it still tastes fine;
verandah furniture. I fade away.
It's time that's lending distance to your view.
I'm watching as you rise and grow in light,
as daylight fades and you and other stars
parade around the cafes, clubs, and bars,
and glister photo chemically past night,
becoming brilliant as you always do.

Goodbye's a lengthy process while you wait
for bonds of chemistry to dissipate.
If love is just another change of state,
no wonder grateful one day starts to grate.

Imperfectly heard love song

I saw you something something when
I said you couldn't something then
You something something stars above
If I could only something love.

You kissed him something something hand
And I won't something understand
Again the something stars above
If I could only something love.

Oh, something something stars above.
Oh, something, truly, something love.

My life in amber

Preserved as I was broken: wings awry;
my legs a spastic cross-hatching, a scrawl;
my abdomen and thorax curve: a small,
eternal question mark of pain. Dead fly.
You wear me on a chain around your neck.
I'm unaware in here of anything.
I don't know if you look at me for more
than any morning's careless making sure
of lipstick, blush, mascara, wedding ring;
the five sec. cursory perfection check.

You take me off at night. I'm not aware.
You place me on the table by your bed
and welcome this day's lover to his share.
Preserved as I was broken, like I said.

A Thousand Things

It must be spring. The pubs are turning into
sushi bars; old women into lanes.
You almost feel the tarmac throb as plane
trees warm their engines. Birds sing, or begin to.
A day, you'd say, that made a great page one.
But nothing starts. It follows. It's a script:
the weather, characters, the funny scenes
when you were younger, casting round for genes
to leave your offspring properly equipped —
but all you leave is all you've left undone.

It feels like spring. My father knows he's dying.
The room is full of flowers and not much else.
A thousand things undone — none now worth trying.
I wish the bloody flowers didn't smell.

A Visit to the Comic's Lounge
for Wendy

Each generation has to learn to say
fuck on the stage and think it meaningful.
Each time it is, and those who know the trick
should stick it out, remembering to clap
in all the pauses left there for applause.
We only learn the things we knew before,
and only know we've lost them when we learn
them all again, and then, we don't recall
quite how it was, but only that it wasn't
this—which shows we're making progress, yes?

I know a joke which goes like this: the sun
comes up and lights the day and everyone,
expecting nothing else, goes into town
and works until, that night, the sun goes down.

You

You cause the day. Your cloudy mornings kiss
my eyes, your soft grey light upon my lips;
the bed clothes stroke my skin like fingertips;
your body warmth is mine, and yours is this:
the sunlight seeping past an edge of curtain.
You populate my garden, morning Eve,
with many-jointed-legged things that spin
and crawl and fly and spawn like thoughts within
a dozy head, like kisses that you leave
on sleeping lips, like something vague and certain.

Your breath is breathing through my lungs;
I feel your gentle rhythm in my heart
and hear your song sung on a thousand tongues
and join the song. You cause my day to start.

My lover's lover's name

for Desdemona, lying

It tastes like foetal blood miscarried
through my mouth, an iron, acrid taste.
It smells like wreaths of flowering human waste,
of menses, menopause, of never married.
I roll that name around my mouth and dream,
in love with something ugly, fierce, and true,
addicted to its poison and its sting,
the snake bite pain of sharing not a thing
again with you, of keeping secret from you.
I mouth it in a long, slow, silent scream.

I wish you well: a deep and slimy hollow.
I wish you echoes: ten for every cry.
I wish you all the blackness you can swallow,
and knowledge of your drowning as you die.

A Landing At Sunset

Her eyes:
You might convincingly look elsewhere
but they drag you back
and drag the puddle depths you stir and muddy
and find you, flapping and gasping.

Her hair:
You might see your first sunset
she colours it a red
perhaps recalling clouds of red-brown kelp
until your eyes dry out of focus.

Her mouth, her teeth, her smile:
You might remember wild games
played in schools,
the never-known companions, images
that flash in silver, disappearing.

Her hands:
You might enjoy their dry touch
knocking you breathless
and slitting you in one move, arse to gills,
scraping your backbone clean.

Her memory:
You might remember sunset now
and hearing first waves,
the mooring chain, the slap against the buoy,
the thought you might be drowning.

God loves us ugly

God loves the ugly, awkward things,
unshiny crawling things.
God loves the mud.
God loves the film of dust, the cobwebbed corners.
Auks and dodos fire love in God as thrilling as the fall
of peregrines on pigeons;
woodlice, millipedes, and things without a common name,
God loves.
The things that move like slime in current are admired;
things whose flesh seems barely to coagulate
are treasured, bring delight, are myrrh.
Things of the night,
things thought of in the night,
things brought to being in the night of other beings,
dark warm soft unholy things, things of no light;
God loves the ugly, awkward things.

I Contact

She lets me touch her honey skin. She calls
it I contact. I call it heroin.
The bathroom basin's full of soaking smalls,
as slippery as veins. I zero in,
and this is what I call success: success.
Her words are soft as floorboards on my spine,
unhinged as kitchen cupboards, wild as soap;
each touch a splintered sharp of Baltic pine,
each kiss the warm, wet, breathlessness of dope.
She says, "Two noes can make a kind of yes."

She lets me touch her. I contact, she calls it.
Her words are warm as something warm. I zero.
The cupboards, doors, the floorboards, walls, a bit
of something warm. A kind of yes. Eyes zero.

It's Pez

She tips her head back when we kiss: it's Pez.
Dispensing sweetness through my mouth she says,
"I love the way you kiss; I love your lips."
My mouth is filled with sugar warmth; she slips
her honey tongue into my mouth; it's nectar,
it's blossom; it's a sudden shaft of light,
a dizziness, a need to hold on tight;
it's sea spray from the bow wave; it's the sting
of salt on skin, a transitory thing,
a butterfly, a butterfly collector.

I hear the fizzing in my head: it's Pez;
it's ice cream soda in a short glass—easy,
take it slow! She kisses me and says,
your 'thank you' sounds like someone saying 'please me'.

Cathedral of Venus

(The smell of nothing)

It's rubble now. The thousands of our hours,
our carving, painting, setting glass—a slew
of rubbish for the peasants to pick through,
and steal the shards of treasury once ours,
once raised and dedicated to our God.
Odd remnants of the walls still stand and trace
our grand design, our folly, our supreme
co-work, the realising of that dream
that tortures and sustains the whole, sad race;
it's rubble now, and turning into sod.

Sod all. The all that's always left us: nought,
the nothing, zero, cipher, zip, the blank,
the everything that we were ever taught
or learnt. Who ever guessed that nothing stank?

Christmas Adam

It's Christmas Eve and everything is shut
except the hole you left. A hole in space.
A hole you're choosing not to occupy
and I'm as scared of you as light is of
its prism. I see you and dissociate;
I shatter into rainbows, make a spectrum
of myself... your wake is human tinsel.
To everything a season: time to shop,
a time to deaden pain, a time to cut
and run. You've got to go. I've got to stop.

The only thing I change is where you're not
and introduce your absence through the streets.
Occasional late shoppers flash past—spots
of neon in the darkness they complete.

My House

The flowers
kick all the vases over
The pictures jump their frames
Clothes
come out of the closet
Water spits up through the drains

The gates
swing free of their hinges
Curtains run off the rails
The fridge
discovers its warm heart
The butch letterbox chews up mail

The snappy new toaster
just crackles—won't pop up
The doormat has started to bite
The saucepans
are all getting heat-rash
The lights have gone out for the night

The Sugar Generation

We drown in Golden Syrup, amber goo;
in sticky pots of liquid fly paper
we dip our spoons and knives, our fingers, too;
as thick as porridge, nourishing as vapour—
the sweet, warm rush of empty kilojoules.
We know that nothing can go wrong, embraced
in honey folds of something that's almost
like teenage love (without the after-taste);
we smell as fresh as morning's buttered toast;
we shine like molten toffee as it cools.

You wouldn't call this living—this is better—
the sugar generation knows its fate:
we're going to die, so let's die someone's debtor—
they'll clear the table when we've licked the plate.

Howard Firkin

Today

(Like every other)

It's just
as well we haven't met
today I wouldn't know what to say you'd say
you're looking well while I was looking
for a café and you'd say I can't stop anyway
smile
and pass the briefest time of day
and goodbye good to meet and I would walk
the other way or cross the street.

Dragged ragged over bitumen
beneath a thousand stranger soles than mine
my shadow's wearing thin avoiding you
too successfully to be trying to.
Pause: amazing all the faces that aren't yours.

Forever

Forever doesn't last much past the night.
It leaves its warm shape in the bed, the smell
of absence on the pillow in its stead.
It skips out at first light and no one grieves.
The hour comes when every clock is still,
when time itself has only time to kill.

Tow Truck

I'm parked. I close my eyes. I wait. It's coming.
Rain oxidising steel, a cruciform,
two roads, one intersection, coming storm,
the wires in the skies are really humming.
I smell the diesel rainbowed on the tar.
The glow of dashboard lights, the radio,
the memories of nights spent waiting for
a big show, slumped against the cabin door,
the ambo, towie, cop unholy trio,
backstage, we wait for screams, we wait to star.

The headlights coalesce and curdle, pass;
another set of heartbeats I forget.
Tonight, no television lights, no glass,
no blood, no flame, no singing flesh. Not yet.

When you're serious about love

(The lonelyhearts website)

When you're serious about
  goat cheese, rocket, and radicchio salad

When you're serious about
  Margaret River vintages

When you're serious about
  mileage and airbags

When you're serious about
  proximity to schools and childcare

When you're serious about
  shopping

When you're serious about
  superannuation and the medicare levy

When you're serious about
  a really good cut

When you're serious about
  mortgage payments

When you're serious about
  your Facebook friends

When you're serious about
  child maintenance payments

When you're serious about
  floor coverings

Howard Firkin

When you're serious about
   varicose veins

When you're serious about
   keeping the finish on your stainless steel appliances

When you're serious about
   your weight

When you're serious about
   your standing in the community

When you're serious about
   what your parents think

When you're serious about
   bathroom renovations

When you're serious about
   cold pressed, extra virgin walnut oil

When you're serious about
   broadband connection speeds

When you're serious about
   love and you're ready to leave it behind.
Sign up. Log in. Type lies. Hit Find.

Fourteen self-explanatory lines

This is the first of fourteen lines that won't
explain the aching beauty of the curve
your bum makes to your thigh or why if I
could choose to be less awkward when I saw
you I'd refuse and take five lines to do it.
I rang you to apologise for being
stupid but apologised for being
instead. You said it sounded like another
line of mine which I denied. I lied.
And so line ten, where nothing is resolved.

Four lines are needed to explain the three
that they contain. The consequence is two
are left alone. If one of them is me,
left here, then that leaves one left there—leaves you.

Firkin's first space walk

The psych test shows I'm one of those they call
divergent thinkers. My movements here, in space
are beautiful; I'm Pina Bausch; I'm all
and nothing; solid fluid; human race.
And that's my craft: not floating, just not falling.
I'm not surrounded, I'm somehow immersed,
reflections on my visor I can't see;
I'm dancing for the last time and the first,
I'm solid, fluid, spastic, balanced: free.
The stars are bird song and the stars are calling.

I don't do checklists: tick. I guess that makes
my choice of occupation very odd:
a spaceman prone to first and last mistakes—
no lifelines and no anchors here, thank God.

Sleek

The quality of water: sleek. Your skin
is poured around your body, smooth as oil,
the flow of air around an aerofoil,
a seal in water, notes as you begin
a gentle scat with bass and clarinet,
a cat before the fireplace: you're sleek,
a silky dress that licks around your hips,
the caramel of glance, the syruped lips
that sculpt your breath to shape the words you speak;
you're smooth as flame, you're soft, you're warm, you're wet.

A muscled movement glimpsed through undergrowth;
a liquid curve, the sway, the swerves, the turns;
the something learnt by each that's known to both:
you're sleek: your body is like oil: it burns.

The sculptor's model remembers herself
NGV 2010

In his hands I was beautiful. He made
my body sunlight. He was hungry for
my form. He tasted me. He made me sure
that it was right that I should be displayed.
I never knew myself like that again.
My husband never liked it—couldn't bear
to think that it was me, that others saw
my body as it was, the one before
the marriage, kids, the daily wear and tear.
And he was right. He didn't have me then.

The thing I most remember is his hands:
the way he worked, the way he touched my skin.
My body was a moment in those hands.
He made me beautiful and I loved him.

One last poem

Where are you now? Where do I send this last
of many? What's become of you/us/me?
I barely perched upon your family tree,
but still, I'd like to think that something's fast:
a memory, a sound, an incident.
Where are you now? I know. That cloudy place,
that place of mists, of postcards from a friend,
of work, of flowers no one thinks to send,
that place where mirrors hold a single face,
where wistful has the force of old intent.

Goodbye. The word 'last' always twists my gut,
but this is something last, the final must:
as fine as smoke, an end of thread that's cut
and curls and falls, a single cobweb, dust.

www.ingramcontent.com/pod-product-compliance
Lightning Source LLC
Chambersburg PA
CBHW032045290426
44110CB00012B/957